A DIFFERENT KIND
OF PARENTING

From the same author

The Family Experience of PDA
An Illustrated Guide to Pathological Demand Avoidance
Eliza Fricker
ISBN 978 1 78775 677 9
eISBN 978 1 78775 678 6

Can't Not Won't
A Story About a Child Who Couldn't Go to School
Eliza Fricker
ISBN 978 1 83997 520 2
eISBN 978 1 83997 521 9

Thumbsucker
An illustrated journey through an
undiagnosed autistic childhood
Eliza Fricker
ISBN 978 1 83997 854 8
eISBN 978 1 83997 855 5

The Teen's Guide to PDA
Laura Kerbey
Illustrated by Eliza Fricker
ISBN 978 1 80501 183 5
eISBN 978 1 80501 184 2

A Different Kind of Parenting

Neurodivergent families finding
a way through together

Written and illustrated by
Eliza Fricker

Jessica Kingsley Publishers
London and Philadelphia

First published in Great Britain in 2025 by Jessica Kingsley Publishers
An imprint of John Murray Press

1

A CIP catalogue record for this title is available from the British Library and the Library of Congress

ISBN 978 1 80501 295 5
eISBN 978 1 80501 296 2

Printed and bound in Great Britain by TJ Books Limited

Jessica Kingsley Publishers' policy is to use papers that are natural, renewable and recyclable products and made from wood grown in sustainable forests. The logging and manufacturing processes are expected to conform to the environmental regulations of the country of origin.

Jessica Kingsley Publishers
Carmelite House
50 Victoria Embankment
London EC4Y 0DZ

www.jkp.com

John Murray Press
Part of Hodder & Stoughton Ltd
An Hachette Company

For all those who won't be going.

For those who tried.

For those who can't.

For those who wish they could.

x

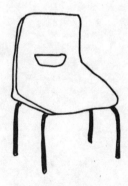

CONTENTS

Author's Note

Like many families, ours has been failed by a system that expects children to follow a very similar and very rigid path. For anyone who falls outside these conventional lines, whether their child is neurodivergent or not, the rounds of paperwork required to access additional support feel labyrinthine. Although I am based in the UK, I know that this problem is one that's experienced the world over.

I started to write and draw when I realised the emails, the meetings, the phone calls and all the formal complaints about the impact that failings were having on my family were, while justified, not changing an awful lot. I just became more upset and cross every time I received a generic reply, and they also took time away from my child when she needed me most.

By capturing how things really felt, I wanted to reclaim our story. I wanted to show others who we were behind the paperwork, with all the humour, wit and disappointment our lives entailed. It didn't mean my frustration went away but it did mean I found a healthier way to vent it and a renewed sense of self-belief. We were more than a system and I wanted people to know this.

While there is no ignoring how isolating those years were, over time sharing my words and drawings created connection, a genuine shared experience with others who were also going through it. As other people responded to my work, it felt like we became stronger together. It was uplifting to know we weren't alone and healing to be able to say, with others, 'It isn't okay that this happened.' We are all different and the products of our own environments and cultures, and we should be valued for this and be able to find our own ways to live and learn safely – a place where we can thrive, not just survive. Our children deserve to have learning experiences that do not traumatise them; there is another way.

Most importantly, this book is here to say that while families should be supported rather than damaged by the system, if and when that damage happens, we can heal and find a way through. If you're still in the thick of things, I want to reassure you that there will be a point, hopefully not too far away, when the past will fade and you can start to look forwards. I hope this book validates the experiences you're having, shows you where some of the glimmers may come from and brings you comfort as you find a way that works for you and your family – whatever that looks like.

Eliza x

Part I

When It's All Going Wrong

Introduction

For so long we try, we all try. Our children keep going to school, even when their distress at the environment spills over to the point of becoming unbearable. Even when it impacts their sleep, food, ability to speak. We keep cajoling, negotiating, bribing, even (as I know I'm ashamed to say I've done) losing our patience with them. Because we know children have to go to school – it is the best place for them, right?

So we keep trying. We have meetings because it's not getting any better. In fact, things get worse, and we start to look around to see where help is coming from. School? Other professionals? This means more meetings, emails, paperwork, wait times. And all of it takes its toll because we are not only managing our children's distress, we are coping with our own anxiety at the same time: the fear of being judged by others, the fear that we're failing our kids, the fear that they're somehow broken and we need to fix them. It is exhausting.

And all of it comes with paperwork and questionnaires and more rounds of 'Have you tried...?' We wake in the night and at dawn, wondering what to do. Worrying over what the future will look like, while trying to figure out the present. Keeping running until there's no road left to travel. In our case, we couldn't go on: we'd tried and tried within the system and it broke us; eventually, we had a child who was too unwell to attend school.

So, in this book we start here, looking at those difficult days and, however hard it is to do, remembering. Because our story is a story that's happening right now, to other families in systems around the world. To those families, I want to say: I see you, and I want to shine a light on your experiences so you know you are not alone.

I hope too that any professionals who are reading this can learn more about how things look from our side, not least understanding the 'double empathy problem', which can make accessing support even more challenging for children and parents who are neurodivergent. (And if you're one of those professionals, thank you for opening yourself up to other perspectives: we need more of you.)

It's only by accepting the past and acknowledging our trauma that we can move forwards and heal.

While the number of children unable to attend school continues to rise, we cannot ignore the system they are struggling with.

Blaming the child and blaming the parents are just distractions.

Taking away phones and making uniforms stricter are not answers.

The numbers are there and rising.

The providers are not providing.

Pressure.

The well-meaning.
The worried.
The wanting to help.
'Have we tried?'
The judgements.
The measurements.
The comparisons.
The targets.
The time frames.
'What about?'
The wait and see.
The no one answers.
The 'you won't get one'.
The vicious circle.
The pressure.
Meanwhile...

Who is on the Special Educational Needs Panel?
Who chooses the Panel?
Who are the decision-makers?

Can we see them?
Speak to them at least?
Can we have a seat at the table?

Did you give them all the documents I sent you?
The things we are never told.
Timelines.
Procedures.

When we don't know things, we feel lost.
Our children's lives out of our control.

No choice and no control.

But clarity; making decisions with the individual and sharing power?
That is trauma-informed practice.
That keeps us feeling safe.

Where are the courses?
I didn't even know I could apply for paperwork myself.

Where is 'an easy guide to Special Educational Needs Departments'?
I've lost days to leaving voicemails in the hope someone picks up or knows the answer.

Where are the 'know your rights' and 'empowering parents' courses?
What about courses on 'masking' or 'autistic experience' or 'improving education for the neurodivergent'?
Where are the autistic advocates?

But I had better go to whatever it is they are running, or they'll really blame me.
Learner? Or Loser?
I blame the parents.

The Believer.
The Trusting.

I was the one who had faith in you, the professional.
Thought you would be our advocate, our support.
It wasn't as bad as I thought, right?
It couldn't be, because you told me so, over and over again.

And I listened.
I believed.
I trusted.

But you watched us fall.
Saw us hit rock bottom.
I know now what I didn't know then.
We learnt the hard way.

We've waited months, years.
I've left messages on a phone that's never answered.
Direct questions.
Generic questions.
Frankly, pointless questions.

You do this and I let you.
(This is the double empathy problem playing out in all its glory.)

You ask me things I don't want my child to overhear.
I mean, we don't know you.
I don't even have your phone number.
But we do this because it might work out, it might help.

Anyway, I've explained it all now, so we'll just see it through
to the end.
We've waited this long.
You never know.

Oh wait, now you've changed the plan.

But that's not what you said!
Well, when?
How long?

I think that's blown it.
I've blown it.

But I'm going to complain, this isn't okay.
Except oh, I forgot, no one answers the phone.

Here we go.

The positive spin.
Whatever was working you are taking away.
'Because they are doing so well!'

Here we go.
Things have picked up, so now it's time to do without.
The Rollercoaster of Support.
The Inconsistency.
The Token Gesture.
Years of Give and Take Away.
Up and then down.

But what you forget is one good day or week doesn't mean my child is 'cured'.
They don't stop having needs.
They don't stop being autistic.

I know, they've been doing really well recently. That's because we had a teaching assistant, but now you are taking them away.
Are you not going to write that in the report, then?

Here we go again.

RECOMMENDATIONS
FUNDING
SUPPORT
ASSESSMENTS
EHCP
TAs
Oh no... Here we go again!
But she's doing so well!

What you don't see is dinner being made several times and still not being eaten because I bought the wrong brand of sauce and the pan tasted lemony.
What you don't see is that I sat up half the night trying to help them switch off (yes, they do have a bath and bed routine).

You don't see that their shorts have been washed and this has tipped them over the edge.
You don't see the extreme meltdowns.
You don't see the shutdowns.
You don't see the tics.
You don't see the insomnia.
You see parenting courses, coffee mornings and an anxiety workshop.

You see a game of Uno with their favourite teaching assistant twice a week.
You see them tick that afternoon registration.

You say, 'They are fine when they are here.'
But what you don't see is the part you need to know. My child is not okay.
It isn't won't, it's can't.

So please don't talk about attendance or resilience, because even with those reasonable adjustments you've made, they are just about surviving.
We are all just about surviving.

And you never see those looks I get at reception when we turn up late again.

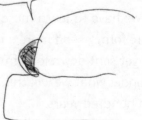

Trudging for days for supplies, gaslighting, sent to the mad-house, begging bowl.
'Please sir...'
But we are not in a Hogarth painting.

Years and years on waiting lists, trying to get the right support.
Court cases (I mean, actual court cases!).
Other people saying they know what is best for our children.
Printouts for support.
Sitting in corridors.
No school.

Be more resilient.
Toughen up.
Get on with it.

This is some of it.
This is what diagnosis can bring.

You think the parents are mentally unstable? Piling it on a bit thick?

So we have to learn more about laws and rights, and fill in more forms, send more emails.
We get sent down long fruitless paths to not a lot.
I wonder what we will think about all this when we look back in a hundred years.

As parents we go through the process of diagnosis because we think it will open gateways of support for our children.

However, after years in the system, we learn that this isn't true.

Those who can provide support rely on parents not knowing the laws or pathways that should be available.

I guess they think that if they offer something to one family, we'll all be asking for everything, but most of the time we are too upset, too exhausted, too overwhelmed by the paperwork.

We're not asking for everything. We're not after a free meal ticket.

If we were, it would be the worst meal ever (like an under-cooked burger or a tinned meat pie).

Please can I look at your big pile of paperwork and see what you say about us?
Please can you ask me what we want or need?
(I can tell you right now how things are at home.)

Please can you tell me what the actual procedure is?
Just don't give me another questionnaire.

Please don't ask me if I want to meet again, because I don't get paid for this.
Please remember that I don't want to be here dealing with this, either.

But for now I simply smile and say thank you.
(Because it's better than nothing and I don't want you to take it away. You never know, it might all mean we get seen more quickly next time.)

PLEASE DON'T SAY

What do you say about me?
When I'm worried that my child has been sitting in a corridor
for weeks on end.

'Mum's very highly strung.'

When you talk about the importance of your job and your
workload, and the number of children you have to deal with,
and I break down because I know you won't help us.

'Mum was verbally abusive.'

So I have to be nice, because I don't know what else you've
written down.
Assertive could become 'rude'.

So I am amenable, not too knowledgeable.
I nod my head to your all-too-obvious suggestions.
I say thank you for the leaflets.
And I smile at the scraps you offer.
(Because we need whatever help we can get.)

I smile.
I go to another meeting.
And I smile.
And we carry on with it pretty much the same as it ever was.
And I smile.

JUST RIGHT

'Mum's just really anxious.'

So that's that then?

Able.   No problems in class
Finds change difficult.

Mum extremely anxious.

Dislikes - sports day.
        - sports day issue.

Hides her feelings.
Just Right programme.

I went to meetings, I hoovered, nodded my head, I listened to 'professionals', I hoovered, I talked about my child to people I had never met before and would never see again, I hoovered, I sat with other parents in the park and listened to their weekend plans, I made sure I had the right foodstuffs, I went to coffee mornings, I hoovered.

I didn't want to be blamed and I didn't want to be judged. Other children went to school, other children could be helped.

She contradicted expectations sometimes, surprised us all, so maybe it wasn't that bad?
But why didn't she want help?
I didn't know.

Maybe it was my fault?
So I hoovered.

don't be late, remember to answer emails, must hoover, don't cry,
ring my mum, follow up meeting, get the right cereal, see if socks
are in the wash tub, change beds, stay polite, be funny, stay calm,
get eight hour's sleep, get teeth brushed, read documents and sign,
write list of questions, take cat to vets, sort out weekend plans,
make packed lunch, buy birthday present, don't forget swimming,
don't be late, remember to answer emails, must hoover, don't cry,
ring my mum, follow up meeting, the right cereal, see if socks
are in the wash tub

PERFECT

te, be funny, stay calm,
get eight hour's documents and sign,
write list of q weekend plans,
make packed lu et swimming,
don't be late, re er, don't cry,
ring my mum, foll , see if socks
are in the wash t unny, stay calm,
get eight hour's s documents and sign,
write list of ques out weekend plans,
make packed lun 't forget swimming,
don't be late, rei st hoover, don't cry,
ring my mum, fol cereal, see if socks
are in the wash be funny, stay calm,
get eight hour's documents and sign,
write list of que out weekend plans,
make packed lu 't forget swimming,
don't be late, r st hoover, don't cry,
ring my mum, f cereal, see if socks
are in the was e funny, stay calm,
get eight hour documents and sign,
write list of q ut weekend plans,
make packed lun t forget swimming,
don't be late, rem ust hoover, don't cry,
ring my mum, follc ht cereal, see if socks
are in the wash tu ite, be funny, stay calm,
get eight hour's sle read documents and sign,

MUM

write list of questions, take cat to vets, sort out weekend plans,
make packed lunch, buy birthday present, don't forget swimming,
don't be late, remember to answer emails, must hoover, don't cry,
ring my mum, follow up meeting, get the right cereal, see if socks
are in the wash tub, change beds, stay polite, be funny, stay calm,
get eight hour's sleep, get teeth brushed, read documents and sign,
write list of questions, take cat to vets, sort out weekend plans,
make packed lunch, buy birthday present, don't forget swimming,

What do we become?

Most of the time we just keep quiet.
We have so much to say but we keep it to ourselves.

But sometimes we just have to get it off our chests.
We need to share our experiences of the maddening systems
we are dealing with, that terrible week of nonsense that con-
sumed us.
Waffling sentences of abbreviations and fragmented phrases.

And then once we start, we can't stop.
I mean, where do you stop?

(I used to talk about books and nice things.)

THE BORE

'Have you tried a visual timetable?'

Sometimes you just want to talk about how it really is, but it is always about a solution, it is always about fixing.

I just wanted to talk about how lonely and worried I felt that holiday but apparently all of life is fixable and it usually involves a whiteboard.

FIXING

Part II

How We Could Make It Better

Introduction

When we begin having to ask for help, we turn to those who work in the system, whether that's education, health or social care providers. Most of us don't have any prior experience of navigating complexity when parenting, so we ask those who do. We hope that they will guide us and advise us on what we need and what will help our child. We share our concerns that things are not getting better. All too often, we're offered leaflets, coffee mornings and lots of generic advice but nothing that gets to the heart of the challenges we're facing.

As things at home deteriorate, the search for targeted and professional input becomes increasingly desperate – but it's usually unclear where help can even come from. In the end, parents and carers resort to sending emails to one and all, in the hope that someone will get back to us.

We jump at every meeting just because it is someone to talk to – even if we're not clear who we're speaking to or why. Even if we end up repeating our story over and over, at a cost to our own energy levels, sense of self-belief and ability to look after our child.

But imagine a world in which parental training courses focus on how the system works, so that we can properly access the support we need. Imagine understanding different job descriptions, so it is clear who does what and so we can attend meetings prepared to make an effective plan. Imagine a joined-up system that takes the onus off families to seek out support and saves us from telling our history again and again.

Imagine a world in which we're told that school is not the only way, that there are other families just like us. Where we don't need to use outdated models of 'support' that neither fit nor work for our children. Where we're shown options for different learning environments that are child-centred and trauma-informed, and that don't require tons of paperwork and court cases.

I hope that the reflections covered in this section cause everyone, families and professionals alike, to start thinking about what a better future could look like – and how it could be made to happen.

You feel in your gut.
It's an inner sense.
This isn't right.
We are not sure what yet, but it's a feeling.
None of us feel good.
This isn't okay.
They are not okay.

I don't have much but I have this.
I know them, inside out.
Intuition.

'We are aware of the difficulties your family...'
'As you are aware, due to...'
'As far as we are aware...'

Support must come from consistency and investment in families.
In individuals feeling they can trust, then share.
In safe spaces to access when they need to.
Feeling wanted and heard.

I am not aware of anyone getting this from a checklist.

We didn't find a landscape of learning and discovery post-diagnosis. Because we didn't get courses on anxiety, masking and burnout.
We didn't get to hear first-hand experiences.
We were just told 'It will be fine' and 'They will be fine'.

How will it be fine? How can it be?

We need to share knowledge and we need honest conversations. Because being given sticking plasters and blinkers and head tilts is not enough.

Our children are going to a place every day that does not feel calm or safe.

Yes, some of us eventually get a scrap of paper to describe needs, but what value does it hold if we do not have true understanding?

You can schedule in some sensory breaks (that my child won't take because it will make them stand out from the other children). You can give them some colours to point at to say they feel mad or sad.

But really we should start by trying to understand what an average day is like for our kids.
It is time we start making some really big changes from the ground up.
Because it is not fine.
Our children are not fine.

The thing is they hit you where it hurts.

'What about friends? Don't you want to give them the best chance?'

No one wants to see their child struggle, so you accept the offer of training courses.
How to be a better parent.
How to have a better child.

Someone is telling you (ever so nicely) that there is a better way to do it.
Because then your child will go to school.
Then your child will be like everybody else.

Behaviour strategies sneak in everywhere. Parent groups, special schools, support groups, coffee mornings.

'Don't you want them to succeed?'

Yes.
I want them to grow into who they want to be, whoever that is.
I want them to be themselves.

You and I are different (maybe you like weddings; I hate them) and that is okay.

What is not okay is teaching children to pretend to be someone they are not.
What is not okay is training them to change or fit.
Change the environment, not the child.

THINGS TO LOOK OUT FOR...

SOCIAL COMPETENCY

Social Skills for Children

IMPROVE QUALITY OF LIFE

Non-Abusive Psychological Intervention

Have you seen the place?
It's like a beautiful stately home.
(That'll please the grandparents.)
It even does horse riding.
It looks like it's meant to look.
It ticks the boxes.
And 'they' all want the answers.
A quick fix.
A solution.
But I don't think that swanky building is for us.
Because it's an advert, it's selling an aspiration.
A goal we can't ever quite reach.
(We've all seen those Christmas ads.)

But that's not us.
We left that behind a long time ago.
When we realised it was going to take more than 'the same but smaller'.
Not more training.
Not more micromanaging.

We needed flexibility.
We needed different.
We needed a total rethink.
So I shed the expectations and we found our own thing.
We found kindness, emotional consistency, those who 'just get it'.

It's a lot nicer really, but it doesn't look like the brochure.
(I actually have a few ideas for my own advert but I couldn't stand to see the faces in that pitch meeting.)

Special.
Different.
Other.

Imagine if instead of learning how to hide who they are (until they break), our children were reminded of what they can do more than what they can't.

Imagine if instead of 'fix to fit', we had options and flexibility, and made adaptations that worked for everyone.

Strengths-based learning, interest-based learning, emotional consistency, connection, autonomy.

What if learning put as much importance on feeling confident and safe in who we are and on finding out about how we learn, work and relate to others?

Maybe then there would be less need for 'special', 'different' and 'other' and more for 'all'.

1900s

2000s

Unit/hub? Sift/separate? Equal/different?
Adaptations, to a point.
I guess it ticks the attendance box.
I suppose it has a beanbag and some fairy lights, although you'd rather be doing DT with your friends.
Inclusion or separation?

I tell you that you were born who you were meant to be.
I tell you to be proud of your creative, funny, bright and sensitive self.
I tell you to be yourself.

We could make schooling flexible and smaller and more individualised for everyone.
We could relax on the whole nylon blazer and traffic-warden school shoes.
We could explore an interest-based curriculum.
We could spend less time on diagnosis and more time on personalised responses.
We could have fewer children standing out for their differences.
We could move to a more progressive way of learning, reflective of the working world.
Or we could just make a room with a beanbag.

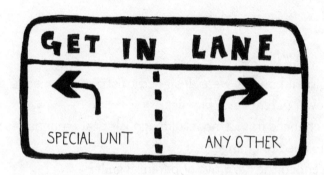

GET IN LANE

SPECIAL UNIT

ANY OTHER

Imagine if courses were designed to share knowledge and empower parents and families?
If we changed from a model of diagnosis that emphasises the child's need to change?
If we ended the narrative of parental guilt?

Diagnosis should be there to inform systems on how to make adaptations. To educate the educators and professionals rather than be a reason to blame or excuse.

If we used our knowledge to work collaboratively as parents and professionals we could create flexible and adaptable learning environments that meet our children's needs.

Imagine an education system that works for all.

I am a woman.
I have a voice.
I have an opinion.

I have many years of lived experience.

I am valid.
I can tell you things.

And when you don't use my name?
You say I am not a woman, with knowledge.
You reduce me.
You invalidate me.

We need to work together.
Hear each other.
Work collaboratively.
Learn.

So please, don't call me Mum.

Dont Call me

Sometimes it's thinking about the end goal and how we get there with positivity instead of shame.

Can we share the load?
Share our experiences?
Talk it through?
Can we collaborate and work alongside to come to fair and rational decisions?

Embarrassment and shame can entrench us.
It is better to feel safe, to see our errors, to learn, to move on.

Mistakes are learning too.

If the outcome can be the same, but we can reach it with less distress and less embarrassment, let's choose that way.

What a difference words make.

What if they said...

Part III

Finding a
Way Through

Introduction

So often, when we seek guidance from those who work within the systems that are in place to support us, they do not come back with clarity, action, support and plans, even after we've shared with them our painful truths. Sometimes what we have said is altered or forgotten. Sometimes our children are hurt, but our concerns are ignored. We are already spread thin and existing in a haze of stress, lack of sleep and immense worry. When things aren't recorded accurately or understood properly we become confused, and it becomes even harder to think straight and access the support we need.

Sadly, for many, a creeping realisation starts to set in that perhaps safeguarding, rules, regulations and correct procedures don't always apply when it matters most. We can see that what our (deeply unhappy) children need is more kindness and flexibility, individualised responses, understanding, co-regulation – but this isn't what's being offered.

Over time, we start to question things more deeply and to ask whether the advice we're being given is actually helping. Our weathered selves learn that we must go back to the drawing board and reassess. So we politely pull back and take stock – because, after all, none of this is working. In the struggle between attendance and scores, and wellbeing and safety, we need to pick a side.

In my case, the realisation set in that I wanted my family back and the only person who could truly make it happen was me. I started to think: this is my job, I know this is something I can do, I just got distracted by input that wasn't helpful. I am going to start doing what we need. And those other voices? They needed to get quieter, so I could get louder. I started to develop the confidence to question authority and identify what would work for our family – even if it wasn't what the system offered or expected.

These steps were hard to take and were wrapped up in insecurity, uncertainty and self-doubt. None of us have a crystal ball, but sometimes it's worth taking a leap of faith. Even if you're not sure what the future holds, if the present and the past are marked by trauma, you may decide it's a risk that you're prepared to take.

For us, it was the start of something new, and fresh, and much, much better. I hope other families can read our story and say 'enough is enough' sooner than we did and trust the process of finding another path.

I chose a side. I chose us. I chose me. I chose my child.

On my walks I would see an old campervan.
They had made it nice, with curtains and pot plants.
I sometimes saw the mother and child who lived in it.
They looked okay, happy even.

So I made it an option.
We could do this!
If it all goes to shit, we could live in a van.

I mean, it had already gone pretty awry.
But at least this made me feel I had some control.

So maybe a van, a wooden hut in the woods, a beach, a remote
town?
We could go anywhere.

Options.
Kept me afloat.
Kept me sane.

Those options may not have had legs, but they gave me space.
They gave us choices when we didn't have many.
As long as we had options, we would be okay.

The Onlookers.

You've got a plan.
It's working rather well.
You feel a lot lighter.
Everyone is happier.

But then come the questions.
The ones you can't answer.

So you wobble.
You get snappy at bedtime.
Because you've let them in.
The doubts.
The what ifs.
The 'normal'.

Right, time to regroup.
Hunker down.
No one needs the raised eyebrows.
It just sends us right off track.

Instincts are often all we've got.
They tell us all we need to know.
They are what our children need.
Don't lose them, don't let them be lost.

This is my job. The one that eats into my sleep, that takes over every conversation. That bores me to tears, that makes me anxious.
I'm not even sure what I'm meant to do or how it all works.
No one answers my emails.
It doesn't have a start or finish time (if they do email it will be late Friday afternoon).
Oh, and I don't get paid for it.
(I did have a paid job once but I couldn't manage it with this one as well.)

I have learnt to treat it like the other (paid) jobs.
I walk the walk, talk the talk.
Don't get me wrong, it is the worst job I've ever had. Everyone ignores me most of the time.
But I know what you need. I've figured this out, we have a plan.

I need to make this work.
Because this isn't about me (I binned that long ago), this is about getting what you need.

With my nicest smile and my hair brushed (that under-eye cream is soooo good) I dust myself off and start again.

I'm going to do this without you ever knowing what a stress it is.
You don't need to know that. I'm going to pretend I like my job.
I'm going to get you what you need.

And if I get any time off, we might even get to hang out and do something nice at the end of this.

I want you to see what you've done. That this is not okay.
I'm mad and I'm really disappointed.
So I keep trying.

All those meetings.
Those emails and waiting, oh the waiting for the phone calls.
('No caller ID! I need to get this!')

I want you to hear me.
I want you to do now what you should have done years ago.
So I keep trying.

But what's it going to achieve?
I've already used up a lot of time.
I want you to see, to change.
But I'm just growing more disappointed.

And this is time I could be with my child.
This is time I won't get back.
This is time when my child needs me.

So I'm not wasting it in another meeting for meeting's sake.
(It just makes me feel depressed.)

There's other stuff I want to spend my time on.
So I'm off to watch telly. I've used enough tokens already on
this nonsense.

You think we want the same things because what kind of
parent would I be if I didn't?
We all know your goal.
School is best.
School is friends.
School is GCSEs.
School is success.
School is future.
This goal (obsession, if you like) of school is yours, not ours.

Our way doesn't come with pomp or ceremony.
We won't have that photo album.
We certainly haven't got those milestones.
I know we don't have what others have.
We definitely don't have it all.

The uncertainty takes a mental strength that on bad days
can immobilise me.
(I learnt ages ago that comparison will actually do you in.)
But then I only need to remember the days before we got here.

So I smile and check in occasionally.
But I keep the knowledge that our Golden Ticket is different
to others.

You can keep your own Golden Ticket, it wasn't what it was
cracked up to be.

GOLDEN TICKET

In your wildest dreams you could not
imagine the marvellous SURPRISES
that await you!

'But what about GCSEs?'
Even if you achieve them, they are not guarantees of a life of
happiness, wellness or success.

'What about a career ladder?'
Back to the swim lane.

So, what if we jump ship?

Will we descend into chaos or will we actually guide our
children in the important lessons, the ones they need most?
Safety, love, consistency, confidence.

I know this, even though I've never worn a lanyard.

I've let you in a thousand times: meetings, phone calls, home visits.
You pop into our lives for an hour, and then you pop off.
You bring your checklists and your generic questions and then you are gone again.

This isn't about my child; this is about evidence for you to say there aren't any needs to be met.
It doesn't make things better; it makes things worse.

My child has learnt to mask in front of authority and you know that but still you come.
There are those who profit from our children, and there are those who believe the system works and our children can be worked on and fixed.

But we can choose to politely decline.

So, I politely decline.
I can protect my child, that is okay.
This is not in their best interests.
I'll do the meetings I need to do, but the rest?

Sometimes it means being late.

Sometimes it means not having another meeting because actually what's the point?

Sometimes it means saying, 'No thank you.'

Sometimes it means choosing what is actually important – important for your child, not important for other people.

Sometimes we need to be able to walk away.

Full of options.

With positivity because we've started to make changes and see the green shoots.

Because this way is breaking us all.

Sometimes we need to be able to walk away.

For our family.

For what we really need.

To a new way.

To nice times.

'You don't care?'

No, I really do, but not about that stuff.

I care about not losing any more time with those that need me.

So I'm walking away.

It's okay, I can fill out another form and write my name, address and date of birth AGAIN.

Sure, I'll tell you everything over the phone for the third time in a month because even though it's a bad story, I've said it so many times now it's more like a script anyway.

Yep, I'll wait another six months for an appointment that will probably be a 15-minute phone call. Oh well, I didn't get your name or department and it was caller ID withheld and I just told you stuff and you promised to follow it up with an email confirmation and you didn't.

No, it's fine, honestly. We can reschedule for next month even though I arranged childcare for today and you cancelled on the morning of the actual appointment.

I thought I had already told you, but now we have to go through all of this again?
Honestly, it is fine.
Because one day I will lie on a beach on a Greek island with a pile of books and glasses of ice-cold rosé.

(Remember that happy places do not expire. You will definitely go there in the distant future. I can't say when exactly – but I promise you'll make it.)

We ripped the rule book up.
It had made us all sad and argumentative and stressed.
But sometimes it is hard to do things differently.
We worry about judgement, about those looks.

What will people think?

But then I remember.
'Does it really matter?'

Curiosity is your way in.
Curiosity is your connection.

We might not eat dinner at the table.
But we choose our battles.

Meetings.
Courses.
Services.
Coffee mornings.
To fix the distress, the shutdowns, the meltdowns, the disengagement, the absences.

Meanwhile, I let guilt swallow me whole.
It must be me.
(Too tough, not tough enough, too many rules, not enough routine.)
My parenting, my ways, our ways.
(I needed a whiteboard apparently.)

My whole family, our existence.
None of them said, 'Oh, could it be us? Could it be this place?'
But when we changed the environment.
School.
It went away.

The distress.
The shutdowns.
The meltdowns.
The disengagement.

And we didn't need courses, coffee mornings, meetings.
We got our happy person back.
(Without ever buying a whiteboard.)

ENVIRONMENT

Some things I treasure
(like those pre-school days when we cooked, read and played).

Some things I put in the bin
(shouting to get to school on time, those sinking feelings
when I let comparison creep in).

But all of these things are learning.

We don't enter this world full of answers.
Most of the time we are winging it, figuring it out on the job.
Nobody knows it all. What works for one might not for another.
(It can't be your way or the highway.)

The world is complicated. We are complicated.
Give yourself a break.
Because we are all learning.
Some of us are further along than others.
But we can share what we know.
We will get it wrong sometimes.
They will get it wrong sometimes.

But change comes from safe spaces, from being able to say
sorry.
Change comes from doing a bit better the next time.
Change comes from thinking, 'I won't do that again.'
Change comes from ignoring unkindness, and from being kind
to ourselves.
Pass it on.

Those same old questions.
By family or friends who don't understand.
By 'professionals' who have immovable markers of 'success' for our children.
They don't know what else to say.

Our journeys highlight the inflexibility of the systems, of the measurements and evaluations.
None of it is helpful.

We lose friendships or move away from relationships as we tire of explaining our children and ourselves.
So we seek kind and supportive relationships; people who don't judge, who just accept.
We learn more about different ways of being, different ways for our children to thrive.
We carve new lives for ourselves, with those who understand.

The future doesn't come from judgement or anger.
It never comes from by making someone feel small.
It comes from hanging out, getting to know each other.
Actually listening.

Sometimes it means having a good look at the past and
saying that wasn't okay.
Saying sorry (always say sorry).
Because we can always do things differently.
We can nod, smile (at that unrequested advice)
and do it our way.
Then, slowly (time, remember, lots of time), the future doesn't
look too bad.

Things get lighter.
We can let stuff go.
We can actually see the future again.

FUTURE

Part IV

Why It's Worth It

Introduction

We reached a point where we were a shell of what we had once resembled and what others had. By then, there was no hiding. We were a wreckage; all broken. We stood, looked and wondered at what had been left. And we stopped.

And when time was all we had, we started to use it differently. We looked back and processed all the rage, the anger, the disappointment, the sadness, the exhaustion. We named them all and wrote them down: they were your words, your feelings. We could do this because we were home, in our safe space, together.

So, if you're at this stage right now: take the time to breathe and look out the window and sit. Sit with your child. It's all I had for a long time, so I took it. Sitting, cups of tea, staring out the window. I even drew the rooftops as they became so familiar to me. I drew and talked out loud to my silent child. Because what we needed was to connect, to get our connection back. So just be there, sit, share.

This was what I started with, and I can't say how long it lasted for because I let time go. Progress was never linear but gradually (so, so gradually) I saw things: glimmers, green shoots. Tiny things no one else would notice, but they were ours. When this happens for you, write them down so you don't forget. Keep those notes for the bad days or weeks, so you can look back and see how far you've come. And don't forget to just sit.

There is no one else who can do this job and you have the best toolkit there is. It is yours, just for your child, and it is filled to the brim with safety, consistency, love and humour. Even when you don't see much happening, stay steady, keep being.

Just sit. It is always about just being. You will get there. Just sit.

Make that time the best it can be with very little. This is what they will remember. They will remember you always being there and that you did it all without resentment, that you made it good and fun. Find the things you need to keep up your energy too: exercise, chatting to friends, walking the dog. Your enthusiasm, you, will be just what they need. You bringing the world to them inside the house when outside is too much. You bringing energy in until they can start to consider looking outwards. All this will take as long as it takes.

You will find that it works for both of you too, this time, this toolkit, this sitting. You will both get there together, forwards and backwards.

It is easy to become suspicious.
To feel it is all not going to work,
Because it hasn't before.
Anger, defensiveness:
These are what can creep in.

So we might micromanage.
Try and control it all.
(I mean, no one wants to fall again.)
This is our own trauma, I guess.

But we need to trust ourselves.
Our children learn the most from us.
So I'm doing this with energy, positivity.
I have nice people over.
I go out and see stuff.
I chat about the not-so-good but then do something else.
Good and better is what I am modelling.
Fun and footsteps forward.
I've let the other nonsense go so I can let the nice stuff in.

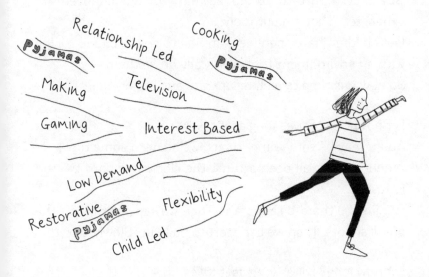

Relationship Led   Cooking

Pyjamas   *Pyjamas*

Making   Television

Gaming   Interest Based

Low Demand

Restorative   Flexibility

Pyjamas

Child Led

One of the hardest parts of seeing our children at home is that they will often spend a large period of time not doing anything.
They will be in their rooms, sleeping, on their phones or gaming.
This can be extremely worrying for parents.

Our children struggled at school and now we watch them, inactive.
But it is important to realise many of our children are exhausted. They are burnt out.
Our children have spent years trying to go to school; coping with an environment that eventually broke them.
So now it is time to rest, recuperate and repair.

For how long? For as long as it takes.
And it may be some time. In fact, we all need some time.
When we have all been against the clock, it is hard to stop. To reset.
But just be there, be constant. Then we can start to see the green shoots. Then we can start to build up. Slowly, slowly.

For how long? For as long as it takes.

Those meetings, the phone calls? They can wait. We are needed elsewhere.
No, it's not okay that this happened to our child.
Yes, I want to shout that from the rooftops.

But right now? I'm needed here. Quietly.
My child needs me, so I drop it all, and I'm there.
For as long as it takes.

Sharing our own experiences.
Hearing the difficult stuff.
This can't be rushed but we are open to it.
However hard it is to hear.
Maybe we start with our stuff.
Maybe we say sorry.
But the stories are important because we need to be able to say it.
And actually it works for both of us.
Because we heal each other.
We can do this together.
Sometimes it starts with one thing like playfulness or consistency.
Then as we repair we can start to share.
Don't try and rush it.
Never fix it; this stuff is hard, I know.
Perhaps it means we will have to do some things differently now.
To heal and start with new ways.
(We are not going back though, that's for sure.)

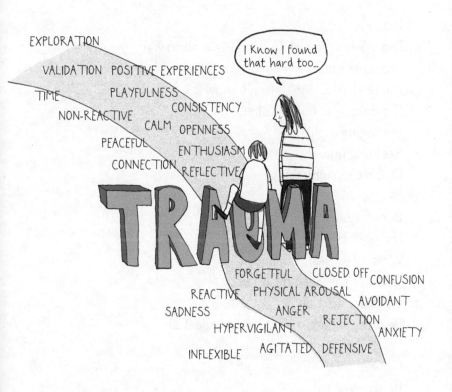

The cryers.
The weirdos.
The crazies.
The 'too emotional'.
The drama queens.

Became...
Those who seem to be carrying it all so well.
The quiet ones.
The ones who don't always show it.
The ones who hold it all in.
Managing it all.
Seeming fine.
Doing the 'right thing'.

Became...
The perfectionist.
Without a fuss.
Without the need of others.
We must do it all.
Because we are meant to manage it all.

Instead...
Be the weirdo.
Think outside the box.
Ask for help.
Share.
Mess up.
Make mistakes.
Start again and again.

Something happened recently and it surprised me because I
thought I was fine.

I fell apart.
And the thing was, things are 'good'.
Our child is happy and well.
But this was it. I had space.
Space to see what had happened.
Space to look forwards.
And what was left?
Who was I? What had we become?
I can be anything now. So I lost myself.
I lost my way.

The cracks had been there for some time.
And we had been so busy trying to do our bits.
We survived but our force shield was left broken.
Exposed.
And I let things in.
Maybe I needed to?
And now I know that impact, that fall out, can happen at any
time.
Usually when there is space.
So we start again.
We are going to build it up.
With fun and love.
A brand-new force shield.

WHEN THE FORCE BREAKS

NOW WHAT?

It doesn't go one way.
Sometimes it's good and we get happy and excited and then the next day it's not.

This is hard to explain.

People say, 'Well, they did it before.'
But maybe before wasn't actually as good or nice as they thought.
Maybe it took everything they had.

Now they don't feel okay about it.
That's okay.
Because we are learning it's about feeling okay first and foremost.
It's learning to say no.

This is progress.
Feeling okay with not feeling okay.
We keep offering, sharing, energy.

Just because it's not backwards doesn't mean it's always forwards.
It ebbs and flows, with a big sense of safety.

But we used to be funny. Have fun.
So I took the stuff that made us, made me who I was (before all this).
I wanted it back, this is who we were beyond the meetings.
Mucking about.
Talking about the nonsense, ridiculing the ridiculous.
This was us.
No one was having those bits.
We were lightening the load.

'But she's okay now isn't she?'
Doesn't mean we go back.
Doesn't mean we do what we did before.
Doesn't mean we start doing it your way.
Doesn't mean any two days will necessarily go the same.
Being regulated is because we do it differently.
We are here because we don't do those things.
Because their strength and wellness lie in being able to regulate themselves with autonomy.
I'm not saying I haven't had to work hard.
To cope with uncertainty.
The maybes.
To shut out the what ifs.
And I still struggle when I meet those who clearly don't get it.
But here? Us? Well, we are in a place we never dreamed of.
Regulated, independent, self-advocating.
It's just we don't get grades for those.

Terrible things happen.
Sometimes over years and years.

There's stuff.
Lots and lots of stuff.
Stuff that makes you sick, sleepless, dizzy, angry, cynical, enraged.
Stuff that makes you sad and really, really disappointed.

Bad things keep happening.
History repeating itself.
No, it is definitely not okay.

So I choose ways to clean it up.
I draw, I weightlift, I muck about.
This sheds the load.
I let those I can off the hook (they didn't know).
I empathise with loved ones (they were trying their best).
I write letters I will never send (screw you).
I stay away from public rants (never helps).
I love a ball slam (look it up, it's the best).

I say sorry too.

Because my child needs me.
They need joy, enthusiasm, hope.
This is what I want to teach.

I still call out the nonsense, but I clear the pathway.
I make it nice for them.

ASEMENT
SCHOOL
FEAR IN
UPBRING G
SLEEPLESS
MEETINGS
HUSBA
FEAR OCAL AU
PAREI
SCHOOL OF
ARS
MOTHERI
WORRY
ORY BIRTH MIS
IDING TEA
FRIENDSH
SCHOO
NGYBEREAVEI
JAL LIRRR

PREGNANCY
RIBUNAL
LIDA ION
G
CHILDHOOD
GH WORRY
RUST MOTHER
CAREER
ITY
IN LAWS
SCHOOL
Y YEAR
STOR
ANDING
BULLYING
ADVICE
ANCY
TANBER
NOSIS

ADVICE SCHO
PARTNER FEA
DIAGNOSIS UPB
SLEEI
MEE
FEAROC
SCHO
MO
WO
BIR

Sometimes we have to start again.
At first it is just being.
Then ever so slowly,
Over time,
Bit by bit,
Side by side,
Little by little,
We add.
This is recovering.
This is repairing.

Our Way.

What worked for you worked for me.

When you needed to repair, we went back to basics.
And it worked for me too.
We stripped back to what we needed, hunkered down.
The focus was you. Only you.
And, it worked for me too.

We went low demand, took away so much stuff and just kept
what mattered.
Low, even tone of voice, non-reactive.

(Remember when even me running for the door was too
much?)
I had to do all these things because your brain still felt really
unsafe.

Slowly, you healed.
Meanwhile, I did too.

And while the world was shut out because it had to be.
We could rebuild it in a way that we needed.
That worked for us.

Perhaps some things didn't actually matter?
Because now?
Now we have regulation, contentment, humour, conversation.
Things we never had before.
We can be unmasked.
Be regulated.
Do it our way.

So, looking back, I know that it was hard to see you fall.
But without it where would we be?
Trying to be all that stuff again?
Faking it?
No way.
It is.
Our way now.

The whatever-works way.
The no-thank-you way.
This is our own way.

All that time of nothing, just food, sitting, being there.
It meant I could actually watch and learn.
From you.
To be just where we needed to be.

Maybe no card.
Maybe no pancakes.
Maybe no flowers.
Maybe no fancy-Dan lunch outing.
Maybe it's not even mentioned at all.

But...
Your encouragement,
Your understanding,
Your gentle nudges,
Your support,
Your consistency,
None of it goes unnoticed.
All of it matters.

Rewards and treats can come in brilliant and unexpected ways.
When you least expect it.
So we'll do it our way.

CERTIFICATE
OF RECOGNITION

This certificate is to award you for your endurance whatever way you got there (on your knees definitely counts) cos you still got there. Your standards and methods are unlike many and we commend you for this.

I DID
MEETINGS
× 125

SIGNED
Missing The Mark

A clever friend once said, 'More parents need to turn away when their children are playing. Stop watching them.'

Trust ourselves.
Trust each other.

The foundation is consistency.
Our emotions, our availability, our communication.
Then you can have risk and autonomy.
This gives strength, to know ourselves.
What we need, what works for us.
To do it our way.
This is strength.

We are always available.
We are stable.
This is security and safety.

No rules, but no bad behaviour?
No, because the environment is right.

We've all worked out what we need.
Through exploration, through having a try.
We talk about it, but we don't judge.
We figure it out. Together.

Healing didn't come from egg timers, access to a sensory diet, a time out card.
It didn't come from books about autism geniuses (people who are just like you).
Healing didn't come from meetings.
Healing didn't come from a home-to-school book.
Healing didn't come from a hub.
Healing didn't come from group therapy or a checklist.
Healing didn't come from people we only ever saw once.
Healing came from watching telly.
Healing came from mucking about.
Healing came from being together.
Healing came from staring out the window.
Healing came from pets, slippers, cushions, sofa.
Healing came from pancakes.

29 months ago I saw you fall.
And I dropped everything.
I gave it everything I could because I knew I needed to do this.
You were ill. Oh my, you were so ill.
It was time for nourishment, not arguments.
It was time for us.

We stopped with the douchebags.
We hunkered down. We started again.
Every bedtime, mealtime, staring-out-the-window time.
We started again.

Oh my, you were so ill.
Slowly it changed. Slowly you came back.
Slowly slowly slowly.

So we started to let people in again.
Think about options. What could that look like?
'Thank you for trusting us with your family.'
I think I can let go.
I did let go.
I mean, it was still slow.
I had to work hard on myself during this time.
But you were ready. You needed it.
We could trust these people.
So now we start a new year and you are well.
Oh my goodness, you are so well.
You have done it.
You want me to go.
And it feels truly excellent.
(But I might need a power nap.)

The Teenager.

'The teenage years?
Oh you've got all that to come!'
How we pine for the cuteness,
The days out, the pliable, the jolly.
The bedtimes, bath times.

But not me. I am not pining.
We did that ×1000.
So no more needed now, thank you.

Now we've got what we never had.
Connections, hanging out, going out.
I even love them sighing.
Cringing.
Wanting me to leave them alone.
I am the most embarrassing person in the world.

I never saw this far ahead.
I could never see this time.
I didn't think it would ever come.
But now?
They can't stand me most of the time.
They are out and about.
The bedroom is a tip, the food is revolting.
There are shoes in the hallway that don't belong here.
The music drifting under the door is awful.
And it feels absolutely excellent.

Afterword

We are in a different place now, a very different place to one we ever imagined.

At first this was heartbreaking – finding ourselves in the after-math and wreckage of eight years of attempting school. The impact was huge, and I was left with a shell of a child who needed full-time care.

I don't share this bit too much because despite writing and drawing 'our story', I keep much of our life private, and that is especially true for those truly bleak and broken moments. I can say that no parent ever wants to see their child crash and burn, but this, unfortunately, is what happens to so many of us. It is the result of continual exposure to high stress – to the point that our children cannot do it anymore. It is trauma.

But it is not just our children who have experienced stress, it is us too. Watching our children suffer; that is trauma as well. And yet there is no time for us to crumble, as everything happens in real time – we have to muster energy from somewhere, because our children need us now more than ever. And while there may be scraps of support out there, wait times can be horrendous and often, ultimately (and I say this while acknowledging that what is possible should be done well), what can other people do?

In the midst of everything, the realisation came to me, as it will doubtless come to many others: this is my time. And believing that was something I took strength in.

I realised: I would do this, we could do this (although ironically, it was actually about doing very little; I just needed time to be with my child. Helping them to heal and in turn heal myself. This period was a time of huge reflection, not only on what we had experienced but on my own life and childhood too. What worked for me growing up? What would I have wanted more of? We were at ground zero and we could start over any way we wanted or needed, so I brought back the playfulness and imagination of my own upbringing. Long holidays at home just mucking about and creating games from very little. Yoghurt pot bowling, hallway cricket, shadow puppets.

I also knew I wanted to say sorry a lot more than I had ever heard from adults I knew growing up.

I knew I wanted to meet my child where she was at rather than where she was expected to be and to do so without shame or judgement. I wanted to offer more security than she needed, hanging out when she wanted without resentment. I wanted to lie in her bed late, late, late into the night and watch my TV shows in the day so I didn't feel I missed out. I wanted to eat comfort foods, making cakes at any time we wanted – even into the small hours, because now our home, our schedule, was ours and how it needed to be.

I learnt so much over this time too – about who we really were, without the constraints of expectation. We both learnt to find our way, find out what we both needed. We were starting over, remember?

And eventually, healing happened. Green shoots, backwards and forwards. Nudges, encouragement, rejection, misjudgements. It all happened, but we bounced back. And now, years on, I am still surprised by my lucid, chatty, sarcastic child. I am still surprised by the piles of trainers in the hallway. I am still surprised by meals and showers and late-night door slams. I love it all. And no, I don't know about exams, careers. But I couldn't be prouder to hear the laughter, chats and happiness.

This is worth more than any grade.